A Story About
TIME

BOOK 1:
Learning about different increments of time
as we grow a garden.

WRITTEN BY
KAIWIN YEUNG

ILLUSTRATED BY
SIJARJAMIL

TIME:
What we do today
makes a difference in the future.
From seconds to hours,
days to months,
seasons to years,
our care and effort is important.

For free educational material
and more fun stuff
please visit our website

TTXME.com
Ten Thousand Method

Special thanks to my little girl, Faith

A *Story About Time*
Book 1 - Learning about
different increments of time
as we grow a garden.

Written by Kaiwin Yeung.
Illustrated by Sijarjamil.

Paperback ISBN - 978-1-922978-02-8
Hardcover ISBN - 978-1-922978-03-5

NATIONAL LIBRARY OF AUSTRALIA

A catalogue record for this
book is available from the
National Library of Australia

Ask your local library to order a copy, so others can enjoy this book too!

Who wants to choose seeds
for the new garden?

Me!

Who can help me
clear the ground?

Me!

Who would like to build
the garden beds?

Me!

Who wants to plant
the seeds?

Me!

Who wants to make
the garden bigger?

EVENING

Who will help me clean
the tools?

We're tired...

You were very helpful today.
Good night, we love you!

SATURDAY

Still nothing happening...

SUNDAY

A leaf!
It's growing!

DAYS OF THE WEEKEND

Who can stand as tall
as the sunflowers?

Not me!

Look at all the other things
growing too!

Who wants to harvest the autumn crops?

Me!

Sunflower seeds,
corn, lettuce,
beetroot and pumpkin!

Who wants to harvest the winter crops?

Me!

WINTER

Carrots, parsnips,
broccoli, kale,
parsley and cabbages.

Onions, asparagus,
peas, broad beans
and turnips!

Who wants to harvest
the summer crops?

SUMMER

Me!

Strawberries, blackberries, blueberries, tomatoes, capsicum, cucumbers, zucchini and watermelons.

TIME

After so many seconds, minutes and hours.
So many days, weeks and months.
So many seasons and so many years.
We cared for our garden for so long
and now it cares for us.

"From tiny seeds we gently sow,
With love and care, we watch them grow.
Days turn to weeks, and months go by,
Seasons change, and time does fly.

Our garden thrives with our devotion,
Nurtured with patience and emotion.
And now our garden, so healthy and fair,
Gives back to us, with bounties to spare."

NEW WORDS: TIME INCREMENTS

Which pages have these important words?

Seconds - just enough time to make a quick decision, like choosing seeds for a garden.
Minutes - long enough to dig a small hole, or remove some grass from the ground.
Hours - long enough to build nice things like garden beds.

Morning - the early part of the day, when we have breakfast.
Noon - the middle of the day, when we have lunch.
Afternoon - later in the day, when school ends.
Evening - when the sun begins to set and the sky becomes darker.
Night - when the sky is dark and we go to bed.

Days - from when the sun comes up and then goes back down. Enough time to build a whole garden.
Weeks - 7 days, which is enough time for new seeds to sprout.
Months - about 4 weeks. Plenty of time for plants to grow big enough for us to eat.

Seasons - different types of weather happen around different times of the year, which allow different kinds of fruit and vegetables to grow.
Summer has the warmest weather.
Winter has the coldest weather.
Autumn is at the end of summer, so the weather becomes colder as winter draws near.
Spring is at the end of winter, so the weather becomes warmer as summer approaches.

Years - long enough for both fruit trees and children to grow big and strong.

Time - we see different things that happen and change over different amounts of time.

Shorter increments of time

Longer increments of time

NEW WORDS: GARDEN PLANTS

Autumn crops
Sunflower seeds
Corn
Lettuce
Beetroot
Pumpkin

Winter crops
Carrots
Parsnips
Broccoli
Kale
Parsley
Cabbages

Spring crops
Onions
Asparagus
Peas
Broad Beans
Turnips

Summer crops
Strawberries
Blackberries
Blueberries
Tomatoes
Capsicum
Cucumbers
Zucchini
Watermelons

1st BOOK SERIES
Educational stories
for early readers
age 4 - 6.

Book 1
Book 2
Book 3

More books at
www.TTXME.com
Every book contains:

- ✅ fun story lesson
- ✅ warm messages
- ✅ pages of academic resources

Book 4

TTXME.com
Ten Thousand Method